What if every person in your organization asked …

The Magic
Question

A simple question
every leader dreams of answering

DAVID COTTRELL

The Magic Question

*A simple question
every leader dreams of answering*

Inquiries regarding permission for use of the material contained in this book should be addressed to:

CornerStone Leadership Institute
P.O. Box 764087
Dallas, TX 75376
888.789.LEAD

Printed in the United States of America
ISBN: 978-0-9819242-8-1

Credits

Developmental & Contributing Editor — Juli Baldwin, The Baldwin Group, Dallas, TX
info@BaldwinGrp.com

Copy Editor — Kathleen Green, Positively Proofed, Plano, TX
info@positivelyproofed.com

Design, Art Direction, and Production — Melissa Monogue, Back Porch Creative, Plano, TX
info@backporchcreative.com

Table of Contents

The Magic Question

"How can I help?"

Isn't that the question every leader longs to hear?

What if every person on your team or in your organization consistently asked you, "How can I help?" What if your team was totally in sync with and committed to achieving your organization's objectives? What if everyone on your team was willing to leave their comfort zone and take a risk to help your team win?

Impossible? Unrealistic? Pollyanna?

Maybe it is expecting too much for team members to ask how they can help you achieve your goals. Perhaps it's far-fetched to think they could care that much about what happens at work. Maybe it is "old school" to think that people want to help an organization succeed. After all, people are just in it for the paycheck, right?

Maybe not.

According to a recent study[1] of more than 17,000 people, less than 10 percent cited compensation and advancement opportunities as the most critical aspects of a job. It seems money is only one piece of the puzzle...and perhaps a small one at that. So what are the other pieces? According to the same study, the top factors that people consider important in a job include stimulating and challenging work, personal accomplishment, a friendly workplace and belief and involvement in the organization's mission.

Most people do want more than a paycheck – they want to feel good about where they work, whom they work with and what they accomplish together as a team. Of course, there are some people – and you know who they are – who don't fit this category. A few are in it just for the paycheck, or perhaps they don't have the same agenda that you do. And some people simply are not in the right job for them at this time in their life. But these people are the exception rather than the rule.

One of the most ignored facts of leadership is that the majority of your team really does care about doing a great job. They care, but something may be holding them back...or pushing them out.

In another recent poll[2], 84 percent of people polled said they intend to leave their job in the next year. That means they must be missing those other, all-important aspects of their job. A popular word used to describe this vast majority of today's work force is "disengaged." It's an interesting way to describe someone – detached, disconnected, cut off. Who wants to spend the majority of their waking hours that way? Why would people consciously choose to be disengaged? Perhaps there is more to the issue of disengagement than that...maybe people are not given the opportunity to engage.

[1] Conducted by PDI Ninth House.
[2] Conducted by RIGHT Management.

If the majority of your team are good people doing a good job who want to be rewarded in ways beyond a paycheck, and you, as the leader, are there to guide them in doing a good job, then why are your results often less than what you expected and hoped for?

Perhaps the cause is external factors – marketplace or regulatory changes, economic factors or a strategic error. However, in most cases, the cause comes from inside the organization. Peter Drucker once said that every business failure was the result of leadership failure. I have found that statement to be true. Whether it is hiring the wrong people, a lack of capital to sustain the business, failure to address marketplace challenges, creating chaos within the organization or just not paying attention – everything falls at the leader's feet.

The team with the best leader usually wins. But what distinguishes the best leaders is typically not competency; most leaders are competent enough to do the job. The best leaders understand how to lead others toward a common goal. They are competent and also passionate, trustworthy, creative and humane. Daniel Goleman, author of *Emotional Intelligence*, says: "After analyzing 181 competence models from 121 organizations worldwide, we found that 67% of the abilities deemed essential for effective performance were emotional competencies. Compared to IQ and expertise, emotional competence mattered twice as much."[3]

Likewise, the Gallup organization found that the single most important variable in employee productivity is the quality of the relationship between employees and their direct supervisors. Marcus Buckingham and Curt Coffman put it this way: "What people want most from their supervisors is the same thing that kids want

---

[3] *Emotional Intelligence*, Bantam

most from their parents: someone who sets clear and consistent expectations, cares for them, values their unique qualities, and encourages and supports their growth and development."[4]

The best leaders have developed skills that help them understand people and know how to get results through the efforts of other people. That is why leadership is complex – because you are dealing with real people, each of whom has needs and desires. The greatest leaders learn how to turn the complex task of dealing positively with everyone on their team into its simplest form.

In its simplest form, leadership comes down to answering six key questions your team members are always asking (whether you hear them or not). These questions are the same regardless of team members' gender, generation, background or position:

1. *What is REALLY important?*

2. *How am I doing?*

3. *How is our team doing?*

4. *Do you care?*

5. *What difference do we make?*

6. *Are you worth following?*

People have a deep-rooted need to know what is happening in your organization, how they fit in and how well they are performing. When you clearly and consistently answer these six questions, your team will work together with energy and enthusiasm. Their talents will be galvanized and directed toward the achievement of a common goal. Morale will improve. Job satisfaction will increase, and turnover will decrease. You will have a lot more fun leading. And, you will earn the right to hear your team ask **The Magic Question:** *"How can I help?"*

---

[4] *Fast Company* magazine.

Some of you may think that this is a book solely about communication. Answering your team's six questions is about more than communicating – it is about *connecting*. It's about meeting the common need of all people…to understand and to be understood. Connecting *involves* people, and when people are involved, they are engaged. When they are engaged, they will give discretionary effort, and that is when you will hear The Magic Question.

You may believe that you are already an expert at communicating and connecting, and ,therefore, this book is not for you. Well, you are not alone in thinking that your communication skills are top-notch. In fact, in one study, researchers asked a group of leaders to rate their personal communication skills. The findings revealed that 90 percent thought their communication skills were in the top 10 percent. Do the math…something doesn't add up! Eighty percent of those leaders believed they were better communicators than they really were. Obviously, their perceptions did not match their reality. I'm not throwing you into that category, but I am saying that most leaders are not meeting their team's basic communication needs.

The bottom line is this: If you depend on results from others, this book is for you. It will provide you with a proven leadership method to create an atmosphere in which your team will want to ask you The Magic Question. It is not about a new leadership strategy. Strategies come and go. What you will learn in this book is tried and true regardless of the strategic focus of the time. Likewise, the principles apply to businesses in every industry, as well as schools, hospitals, churches, even homes.

Successful leaders must earn the discretionary effort of their people, and earning the right to hear The Magic Question is hard work. It would be nice to say, "Abracadabra!" and have everyone on your team begin asking, "How can I help?" Nice, but it's not going to happen. There is no magic in getting to the question, but when you do your part and your team does their part, you will see magical results.

Read, enjoy and apply what you learn.

What is **REALLY** important?

"Things that matter most must never be at the mercy of things that matter least."
– JOHANN WOLFGANG VON GOETHE

Many of Aesop's fables teach us modern-day leadership lessons. One of my favorite lessons comes from the fable "The Fox and the Cat." Here is the story: A fox boasted to a cat one day about how sly and wily he was. "I've got all kinds of tricks," the fox said. "For example, whenever I hear the dogs coming, I know a hundred different ways to escape."

The cat was impressed and humbly said, "Your cleverness is amazing. As for me, I have only one way to escape, and that is to climb up a tree. I know it's not as exciting as all of your ways, but it works for me. Maybe someday you could show me some of your different escape routes."

The fox smiled smugly, "Well, friend, perhaps I'll have some free time one of these days, and I can show you a trick or two."

Shortly afterward, the fox and the cat heard a pack of hounds baying nearby. "They're coming this way!" the cat shrieked. In a flash, she scaled a nearby tree and hid herself in the leaves.

The fox stood there trying to decide which of his many tricks to use. Paralyzed with indecision, the fox waited too long to make his move, and the hounds pounced on him. The moral of the story: Having too many choices can lead to indecision and inaction.

Just like the fox, when your team has too many "important" things to focus on, they become paralyzed and take no action at all. Confusion about what is REALLY important is a major source of stress on your team. This is why your team has to know, "What is REALLY important?"

You may think that the people on your team are totally connected to what you are trying to accomplish together. You may even think that the "What is REALLY important" question is easy to answer because you communicate in numerous ways. After all, you have mission statements, job descriptions, performance reviews, emails, memos, texts, motivational posters, screen savers and many other ways of communicating what is REALLY important.

But all that communication oftentimes muddies the water. In fact, so much communicating is going on and there are so many things coming from different directions that it's difficult for your team to separate the relevant important from the irrelevant trivial. In survey after survey, year after year, regardless of the new communication tools available, a major issue within organizations continues to be communicating, "What is really important around here?"

The reality is that we work in a constant state of change that, unfortunately, creates communication static. As a result, team members become frustrated, thinking, *"We are out of the loop... Things are always changing...I don't know what they want...I'm not a mind reader...The target is always moving...It's hard to figure out what to focus on."*

Leadership is frustrated, too: *"Are you kidding me? Communication is not the problem. I work with my team constantly – train them, discuss results with them, create mission statements, share weekly updates and give them performance reviews. I spend the majority of my time communicating. They just don't listen."*

Both sides could be right. Communication may not be the problem, and communicating more may not be the solution. In most cases, people do not need more information. Much of the information they receive doesn't get read; what they do read is frequently misunderstood; and what they do understand is easily forgotten. That's not a knock on your team. It's just that there is so much communicating going on that what is REALLY important is hard to sort out from the stuff that is not so important. So rather than communicating more, we need to be connecting and clarifying.

Since conditions are constantly changing – a.k.a. moving targets – effective leaders must keep the REALLY important targets in their crosshairs. It is up to you to identify the overriding objectives that will ultimately determine your team's success and keep the team focused on those main things. If the attention and energy of your people is being directed to anything other than the few main things, that attention and energy is being wasted. In fact, if you are trying to get your team to focus on more than three or four main things, you really don't have any main things at all. Wherever you put your focus...that is where you will get results. Part of your value as a leader is in eliminating the clutter – the minor things that can get in the way of the important things.

If the REALLY important things are not crystal clear, each person on your team will do what is comfortable for them to do and the easy/comfortable will trump the important. Likewise, if you have too many REALLY important things for your team to focus on, they will become paralyzed and take no action at all.

THE IMPORTANCE OF EVERYONE BEING IN SYNC

Synchronized swimming, which involves a team of swimmers who perform in perfect synchronization to music, has been an Olympic sport since 1984. It's beautiful to watch but very demanding for swimmers, requiring fitness, stamina and flexibility. As I've watched synchronized swim competitions, I've wondered how the team stays perfectly in sync, especially when they are performing upside down and under water, neither of which is natural for most human beings.

Olympic-caliber synchronized swim teams must work in perfect unison. Every member must know their individual roles, when to perform each move, and how each of them personally contributes to and affects the team's performance. When every swimmer is in sync, the performance is breathtaking. But if even one team member is out of sync at any point, the entire performance falls apart.

The same is true with your team. Synchronization around what is REALLY important is absolutely critical to success. The military calls this "unity of effort" – harmonizing the efforts of different people toward a common goal. When every individual on your team clearly understands what is REALLY important, and all are unified in working toward those goals, their performance will be energizing, spectacular and profitable. But without unification –

when team members are out of sync because not everyone is clear on what is REALLY important – people lose focus and stagnate. Before you know it, forward movement comes to a halt, and lackluster results follow.

How do teams lose sight of what is REALLY important and get out of sync, especially in light of all the communication that goes on between leaders and their teams? The three most common situations that cause teams to be out of sync are confusion, contradictions and fuzzy expectations. Let's look at each of these.

CORPORATE ATTENTION DEFICIT DISORDER (CADD)

If your team is out of sync with what you are asking from them, perhaps it's because they're confused about what you want. A dizzying array of team and organizational objectives creates Corporate Attention Deficit Disorder. CADD occurs when the things you say are REALLY important are constantly changing. One month, your focus is to increase revenue. The next month, the focus is on decreasing costs. Then hiring is the priority, and 30 days later you are focused again on cutting costs. Which one does your team choose to be in sync with? How do they know what is REALLY important?

When your goals are constantly changing, you can count on chaos and confusion…and confusion shared will become confusion multiplied. You may be thinking that changing direction is not necessarily a bad thing, and of course, you're right. Changing direction isn't a problem as long as everyone is on the same page and understands that the change will help them accomplish what is REALLY important.

If your REALLY important things are a continuously moving target, your team will lose hope. Some people will simply ignore the current goal because they've learned from past experience that the goal will soon change anyway. Why bother changing course now when another change is probably just around the corner? Instead of asking The Magical Question, their thoughts are, *What is it that you really want? One day it's this, another that, then something else. All of this can't be important...what is REALLY important around here?*

Ask *Yourself...*

Do I know what is REALLY important?

If someone woke you up in the middle of the night and asked what was REALLY important for your team to accomplish, could you immediately give the correct answer without even thinking about it? How would your team members respond under the same circumstances?

What percent of your time today was spent on accomplishing REALLY important things? What if you improved that by 10 percent? When you make the best use of your time every day, you make more time for the things that are REALLY important.

UNINTENDED CONTRADICTIONS

Contradictions are the enemy of clarity and synchronization. Very few leaders purposefully create contradictions; however, unintended contradictions occur all the time and in many forms. For example, team priorities that conflict with the organization's stated mission, or claiming that people are your greatest asset and then eliminating employee training because you "just don't have the time or money." Another contradiction is continually stating the importance of teamwork while implementing programs and incentives that actually pit team members against each other. Or giving employees performance reviews that are different from what you've been telling them (or not telling them) about their performance. Any of those sound familiar?

Inconsistencies and contradictions will absolutely paralyze your work group. Consider a call-center environment where there may be two primary performance measurements – answer at least 25 calls an hour and satisfy every customer's needs. When a client calls with a problem that requires significant time to resolve, the call center agent must make a decision: *"Do I take the time necessary to satisfy my customer, or should I let someone else handle this problem so my numbers will not look bad?"* Either decision is right...and wrong. What is REALLY important in this situation, and how would that team member answer the question?

A common contradiction in organizations is reward systems that are out of sync with team or organizational objectives. In fact, leaders often unintentionally reward actions that are diametrically opposed to what they want to accomplish. For instance, have you ever asked your best employees to do more to take up the slack for others who are not pulling their share of the load? Do you reward people who are late for meetings with a brief recap? Do you allow unimportant agenda items to dominate your team's time in meetings or conference calls? If you do any of these things, you are inadvertently punishing your best performers and rewarding the lowest performers.

Another example of an unintended contradiction is how you respond to new ideas that may be outside of your comfort zone. Do you reward innovative ideas with sincere thought or shrug them off as quirky brain drizzle? When you reward creative ideas as thought-provoking and potential game-changers, your team will reward you with more ideas. If, on the other hand, you "punish" ideas with cynicism or ridicule, you will likely lose the opportunity to even hear the next idea.

Contradictions are rarely intentional. Why would anyone want to contradict themselves? Yet unintended contradictions happen on every team and in every organization. Your every action creates a reaction from your team…make sure that you are not rewarding what you do not want to happen.

Fuzzy Expectations

As a leader, your time, energy and effort are spread in many different directions. Sometimes you may forget that the people on your team are not mind readers. You expect them to do what you want, but you may not give them enough information to "connect all the dots." Maybe your requirements are too complex, difficult to comprehend or your expectations are fuzzy. When your expectations don't match their perceptions, the team will be out of sync.

I've had the privilege to deliver keynote messages to hundreds of thousands of people at leadership conferences across the globe. At almost every meeting, I ask participants to do a simple yet powerful exercise that demonstrates what can happen when we have fuzzy expectations. Try it with your team:

First, provide everyone with a blank sheet of paper. Then explain that they must follow two very simple rules: They are to do exactly what you say without questioning it, and they are to close their eyes and keep them closed until you say to open them. After you confirm that everyone understands both rules and that their eyes are closed, give them the following simple directions (you follow the same directions but with your eyes open):

1. Fold the sheet of paper in half. (Make sure they do not open their eyes. Do not answer any questions; simply remind them to do exactly what you say.)

2. Tear off the upper right-hand corner of the paper.

3. Fold the paper in half again.

4. Tear off the lower left-hand corner.

5. Fold the paper in half again.

6. Tear off the upper left-hand corner.

7. Unfold the paper.

Then tell them to open their eyes and compare their results with your results. Everyone's paper will look different. It is fascinating... I've done this with a room of 500 people and no two papers will look exactly alike.

There are at least two major learning points from this simple exercise. First, if you depend on your employees' perceptions to match up with your expectations, you will be disappointed every time. Simply telling people to do something is not enough. Every person who did the exercise thought they were following your instructions and doing the right thing; but without a crystal-clear vision, everyone produced a different result. The second lesson is that if you are not explicit about what you want – if you have fuzzy expectations – you will have to settle for what you get. Your team's REALLY important things will always be what *they perceive them to be*, and the odds are that their perceptions will be different than your expectations. If each person is left to do what they perceive is REALLY important, their tendency will be to do what is fun and easy instead of what may be hard and necessary.

ANSWER THE QUESTION, "WHAT IS REALLY IMPORTANT?" WITH CLARITY, CONSISTENCY AND SIMPLICITY

Your team has to know – without a doubt – what is REALLY important, and you must constantly and consistently communicate that message with crystal-clear clarity. It is up to you to develop a language of clarity that they understand so you can achieve the results you want. It is your responsibility to clearly identify what is required – in priority order – to eliminate the stress and confusion created by seemingly contradictory objectives. Then get the team focused, provide feedback along the way and allow them to ask questions for clarification.

Of course, it doesn't do much good to answer the question with your team unless **you** are totally committed to the REALLY important things and walk the talk yourself. Simply stated, your "video" must be in sync with your "audio." What you do must be in sync with what you say.

The best way to create clarity and focus is through inclusion. Include your team in the process of determining what is REALLY important. If you simply tell your team to "get it done" and do not involve them in the process, you will never hear The Magic Question.

Consistency is also crucial in answering the first question; it is a universal human need. Even though we live in a world of constant change, what is REALLY important should not change constantly. You must continually emphasize what is REALLY important. Likewise, what you reward should be in sync with what is REALLY important. The management axiom of "What gets rewarded gets done" is true. That seems so obvious, and yet rewarding the wrong thing is a mistake that many leaders unwittingly make. Concentrate on rewarding the actions and behaviors that are consistent with achieving your objectives.

Finally, your REALLY important expectations must be simple. People need to be able to remember what is REALLY important without giving it much thought. They work best when they have a few simple, memorable objectives to pursue. Simplicity is achieved when an idea is stripped down to its core, to the most essential elements that make it work.

Simplicity liberates your team. Simple does not have to mean short, but it helps. Great wisdom can be stated in four words or less: *This too shall pass. Nothing ventured, nothing gained. In God we trust. Let sleeping dogs lie.* These are examples of how a complex message can be delivered through a few simple, memorable words. If it takes you more than 30 seconds to state what is REALLY important, it's probably too complex.

To help you simplify what is REALLY important, as a team, answer three basic questions:

1. Why are we on the payroll – what specific, measurable results have we been hired to achieve?
2. What value do we add to our organization?
3. What are the most important activities we must complete in order to provide that value?

When you answer those three questions, you will simplify your message, clear out the clutter and eliminate any confusion about which things are REALLY important. Your team will be energized and more productive when they have simple, crystal clear, memorable priorities to pursue.

Q: Does your team know what is REALLY important?

A: Give each team member a sheet of paper and tell them to divide the paper into three columns. At the top of each column, have them write "Customer," "Organization" and "Me," respectively. Then consider some of the issues your team regularly deals with, such as customer service problems, implementation of new technology, price increases, change of policy, etc. Under each column, ask them to write down what is the best outcome in each situation for the customer, the organization and them as a person.

You may discover that what is best for the customer is not best for the team member, or what is best for the organization is not best for the customer. How should team members determine and prioritize what is REALLY important? Who comes first? The purpose of the exercise is to discover if you have contradictions so you can address them up front before a decision has to be made by the team member.

Answer the First Question:
What is REALLY important?

○ Know your REALLY important objectives. Write them down, talk about them, understand what they mean and let them guide your decisions. Keep your REALLY important things REALLY important!

○ When every individual on your team is in sync with what is REALLY important, they will be focused and move with unity of effort toward a common goal.

○ If what is REALLY important in your organization is constantly changing, you have created Corporate Attention Deficit Disorder, and you can count on chaos and confusion.

○ Unintended contradictions will paralyze your work group, bringing progress to a screeching halt.

○ If you depend on others' perceptions to match your expectations, you will be disappointed every time.

○ Answer the Question with Clarity, Consistency and Simplicity

   ● Clarity: Your team has to know – without a doubt – what is REALLY important.

   ● Consistency: What is REALLY important should be in sync with what you reward.

   ● Simplicity: People work best when they have simple, memorable priorities to pursue.

When you answer the question,
"What is REALLY important?"
your team's performance will be focused
and energized by their unity of effort.

How am I doing?

"Feedback is the breakfast of champions."
— KEN BLANCHARD

The second major source of stress for your team, after confusion about what is REALLY important, is not knowing – from your perspective as the leader – how they are performing. The main reason why performance problems exist is because of poor or insufficient feedback. Leaders often mistakenly think that performance problems are competency or motivational issues, when in fact the problem is a lack of feedback.

Your team is constantly asking the unspoken question, "How am I doing?" Believe it or not, people want feedback. No one likes to work hard and then be surprised to discover that all of their work was for naught. Everyone is insecure to a certain degree and needs to know that they are on the right track.

Almost every car and smartphone now comes with a global positioning system (GPS) installed. Its primary function is to keep you on course so that you can reach your destination safely and as fast as possible. For the GPS to serve its purpose and provide value, it must be turned on. Otherwise, it's just taking up space. Then it has to be programmed with your current location and your destination. When you provide the necessary details, it will show you the best route. And if you should get off course, it will tell you what adjustments to make and when to make them.

As the leader, you are the GPS for your team. If you know the current situation and have a crystal-clear understanding of where you are leading the team, you will move your team toward the goal. Just as important, you will be able to guide them to make adjustments when they get off track. But if you are not turned on and plugged in to your team, you may just be taking up space.

So how do you turn on your leadership GPS and keep your team on track? By coaching your people.

The root meaning of the verb "to coach" is to bring a person from where they are to where they want to be. It is your responsibility to let every person on your team know how they are doing. If they are doing things right, then reinforce that behavior. If they have gotten off course, let them know what they need to change in order to improve. You are the coach; you are the GPS.

Everybody needs a coach – even your best performers. The greatest athletes in the world have a coach, even in individual sports. A coach sees things from a different perspective and can suggest minor adjustments that will yield far greater results than the athlete could make on their own. Your best performers are no different. Certainly, they don't want or need you telling them what to do and how to do it. They are, after all, your top performers. But they also do not want to be ignored. The fact is that many top performers go to bed hungry at night – hungry for feedback and recognition from you. Even though they may not admit it, they need and want to be coached.

The Myths of Coaching

There are a few myths about coaching that need to be debunked up-front. The first is that people do not want to be held accountable. Your best performers want to be held accountable – that's part of the reason why they are your stars. Your lowest performers probably will not be keen on the idea. Hmmm…I wonder why? But in the end, everyone wants *everyone else* to be held accountable. Bottom line, without accountability, you will never be able to move your team forward.

The second myth is that coaching is solely about working with your lowest performers. Not true. Coaching involves staying in touch with everyone on your team – especially your best performers – and providing them with information to help them get where they are trying to go.

Another common misconception is that silence on your part sends the signal that your team is doing just fine (as in, if they weren't doing well, you'd be sure to let them know). Your silence is loud. It definitely communicates to people, but it may not be communicating the message you intend to send. Every team member needs your active feedback to know how they are doing.

The final coaching myth is that by providing formal performance reviews every six months or once a year, you have coached enough and given enough feedback. That would be like a football coach only coaching when the season is half over. Sounds sort of ridiculous, doesn't it? But that is what you are doing if you provide feedback only at review time.

Formal reviews are important but not enough, because they rarely change long-term behavior. An employee's behavior may change a few weeks before the review – as in, "I want my manager to have a fresh memory of the good things I'm doing." And behavior change may last a few weeks after the session: "I did pay attention to my manager's guidance." But, in general, performance review improvements don't last until the next performance review. Long-term behavior change occurs only if the leader, like any effective coach, consistently reinforces the behaviors required to be successful.

ANSWER THE QUESTION WITH COACHING

Here are five tips on how to coach your team and answer the question, "How am I doing?":

1. The most important element of coaching is candor – true honesty about the way things are, not the way you want them to be. Coaching with candor clarifies what needs to be done to improve, while a lack of candor can lead to even bigger problems down the road. Candor also prevents surprises...when you are honest with your people, they will be honest with you.

   Rather than talking around the matter, be direct and speak to the matter at hand. Remember that you are not addressing a problem with the *person*; you are addressing a *situation*. There is no reason to beat around the bush, afraid of offending someone – a situation cannot be offended. Focus on the situation and leave out personal issues.

2. Coaching is a two-way process that involves talking and listening. Both functions are of equal importance and should receive equal attention. In fact, the better listener you are, the better coach you will become. Remember that what matters is what the person hears, not what you say. Don't depend on perceptions – check frequently for understanding.

   Although personal interaction is best, email and text messages are okay for some things. But, once again, what matters is what employees read and how they interpret it, not what you write. Keep in mind that words make up only a small percentage of communication, while nonverbal cues make up the majority. Be crystal clear in all your communication and leave as little as possible open to interpretation.

3. Coaching is not limited to formal reviews and coaching sessions. Let your team know frequently how they are contributing and what they can do to improve. Spend time with your team...the more knowledge you have of what is going on in their world, the better your feedback will be.

4. Stretch your team members – confidence is active feedback. Show your confidence by allowing them the opportunity to stretch their thinking. Encourage them to teach and coach each other. Those who teach, learn more – a win/win for all.

5. Give your team members freedom and avoid micromanaging them. If you answered their first question, "What is REALLY important?" then they know what to do. Give them the freedom to get it done.

Ask *Yourself...*

How are my people doing?

Set aside time every week to quietly think about each team member individually. This simple act forces you to pay attention and gives you the opportunity to provide constructive feedback.

COACHING INVOLVES ENCOURAGEMENT

While it seems that much of coaching focuses on performance improvement, recognizing your team members for a job well done is equally important. Just as a GPS lets you know that you are on course (for example, "Continue on I-75 for 10.2 miles"), everyone on your team needs positive reinforcement that they are on track. Encouragement brings out the best in people. Effective leaders are encouragers who push their team to move in the right direction.

If you are like most leaders, you are fairly confident that you do a good job providing encouragement. However, studies show that there is a significant difference in the perceptions of leaders and their teams as to how often positive feedback is given.

In one extensive survey[5], leaders were asked to respond to this statement: "I let my subordinates know when they are doing a good job." The subordinates responded to a similar statement: "Leadership lets me know when I'm doing a good job." The same question but from different perspectives. A scale of 1 to 5 was used, where 1 represented "never" and 5 represented "always."

The leaders rated themselves a 4.3. In other words, the leaders thought they almost always let their team know how they were

---

[5] *Managing the Equity Factor,* Richard Huseman, John Hatfield, Houghton Mifflin

doing. But the employees gave their leadership a 2.3. What a huge gap in perceptions! Based on the results of this study, we can assume that for every piece of positive recognition or feedback leaders give, they receive only "half credit" with employees.

Who was right or wrong in this survey is not the issue…and neither is how much positive feedback you actually give. The point is that it is your team's *perception* that counts. Don't allow yourself to be fooled into thinking you recognize positive behavior too often. Do it twice as much as you think you should, and you will have a better chance of meeting your team's needs.

Your team also needs specific, detailed feedback. General encouragement alone is not enough. Does a GPS say, "Continue on" or "Turn left at the next road"? No, it provides explicit details: "Continue straight for 0.6 mile" or "Turn left on Highway 360 in 1.7 miles."

Lorraine Grubbs, former Southwest Airlines' executive, shares one method used in Southwest's coaching training to reinforce the value of specific coaching: "We divided our group into three teams. One member of each team was blindfolded and asked to throw a ball into a trash can. Unknown to the throwers, the members of one team were not allowed to say anything to their thrower. The second team's members were allowed to encourage their thrower, but they could only say 'good job' or 'keep trying.' The third team could give detailed information to their thrower about where the trash can was and how their ball was missing the can. Not surprisingly, the third group had the most success. The other two teams' throwers were frustrated and lost hope of ever hitting their target, because the feedback they were getting was not helping them get closer to their goal."

This simple exercise teaches that coaching is more than giving instruction and giving encouragement. Effective coaching is specific in directing them to their goal.

Your team continually wants to know how they are doing. Coaching is an on-going process where every interaction is an opportunity to clarify goals, prioritize tasks, provide specific feedback and offer positive reinforcement.

Q: How well are you providing feedback to your team?

A: Try this quick exercise to find out:

1. While working in a private area, write all of your team members' names on a flip chart or piece of paper. Arrange them in order from the top performer in your mind to the person you perceive to be your lowest performer.

2. Gather all the most recent performance reviews that you've completed for your team. Post those review scores by each individual's name.

3. Check your personnel files for all the members of your team. Place a check by the name of each person for whom you have provided documented, positive recognition.

4. Again, retrieving information from your personnel files, place an "X" by the name of each person whom you coached for performance improvement.

5. Take a look at your list. Is there a difference in the feedback you are providing the best performers and lowest performers?

Several years ago, I completed this exercise and discovered that if someone did not know the names on the list, they would have no idea who my top performers were. The best performers' reviews, recognition and performance coaching were not significantly different than those for the lowest performers. I realized I was the problem. I had not answered my team's second question: "How am I doing?" Everyone assumed they were doing fine, which was totally wrong. My best performers were doing great and my worst performers were not meeting my expectations, but neither group knew it.

I hope you will do this exercise and discover that you are not making the same mistake I was. But, if you are, have the courage to begin coaching your team today. It will change everything!

Answer the Second Question:
How am I doing?

○ Not knowing how they are doing from your perspective as the leader is a major source of stress for your team.

○ Make sure you have installed and are operating your team's GPS. Let them know where they are, where they are going and what route they need to take to get there as quickly as possible. Then guide them in making adjustments if they get off course.

○ Everyone needs a coach – even your top performers.

○ People have a need and desire to be held accountable.

○ Silence is not active feedback. Everyone needs positive reinforcement and to know that they are doing okay.

○ Formal performance reviews are not enough. Every team member needs to know more frequently – much more frequently – how they are doing.

○ A two-way process of talking and listening is essential to effective coaching.

○ Catch your team members doing something well and celebrate with them. Give recognition and positive feedback twice as often as you think you should.

○ Your team needs specific, detailed feedback rather than general encouragement.

> *When you answer the question, "How am I doing?"*
> *your team will achieve positive results*
> *and reach their goals faster.*

How is our team doing?

"The leaders of winning teams always – always –
let their people know where they stand."
– JACK WELCH, *Winning*

Everyone likes to win. From the time you won your first game in soccer, volleyball, baseball or any other sport, you naturally learned to enjoy the feeling of winning. It is energizing when a group of individuals sets a goal and achieves it. People you work with are no different – they want to be part of a winning team. Individual goals, expectations and feedback are important, but people also want and need to win together as a team.

Your role as the leader is to define what winning means, eliminate any obstacles preventing the team from winning, keep score and coach the team appropriately based on the score (either celebrate or make adjustments). In other words, you need to answer the question, "How is our team doing?"

Everyone wants to know if their team is winning. No one wants to find out they've been losing all along but didn't know it. The key to answering the question, "How is our team doing?" begins with the leader sharing knowledge. The more knowledge you share about how all the pieces work together, the more confidence and power you give your team.

KNOW THE SCORE, SHARE THE SCORE

How can you make sure everyone knows how the team is doing? Start with a thorough understanding of exactly what the team is supposed to be doing. Then measure what matters and monitor it on a regular basis – in other words, know the "score." And finally, make sure that the "scoreboard" is always on, providing consistent visibility of how the team is doing. This is the only way everyone will know, without a doubt, whether or not they are winning.

Every team and organization has numbers that measure if it is on track (the score). Those numbers could be sales, turnover, new customers, loss of customers, business referrals or some other internal performance measurement. Whatever it is that you measure and monitor should not be a secret to the people on your team. The numbers are more than digits on paper – they are business gauges that measure results and determine success. They are the truth about the business, and everyone needs to know the truth. When your team knows the score, they stay focused on what is REALLY important.

Some of the best years of my career were spent working at FedEx. It was a dynamic, growing company with great leadership and a true emphasis on teamwork. FedEx was committed to continuously measuring how each team was doing and sharing that information with everyone. I believe this measurement system provided the foundation for their outstanding service.

Customer satisfaction was not only a passion for FedEx, but a business necessity. Many organizations measure the score by the percentage of satisfied customers, and most are happy with 95 percent customer satisfaction. At FedEx, 95 percent wasn't good enough (and neither was 99 percent). Ninety-five percent customer satisfaction meant that 150,000 customers would be dissatisfied – every day. Can you image dealing with 150,000 dissatisfied customers every day?

Fred Smith, CEO of FedEx, believed that while all customer failures are bad, the worst ones were the top priority. His philosophy was that customer issues should be monitored and addressed in accordance with the severity of the failure. For instance, any package delivered late was a service failure, but a delivery that was late by minutes was not as damaging to the customer as a delivery that was late by a day or more – that was a service disaster.

To measure and monitor their service results, FedEx created the "Hierarchy of Horrors" (later renamed the Service Quality Indicators) to identify each type of service failure and then assigned a value to each one based on its impact on customer satisfaction. For example, the three most severe service failures (damaged packages, lost packages and missed pickups) were assigned a value of 10, while less serious problems (such as delivery on the correct day but after 10:30 a.m.) were assigned a lesser value.

Every day, the Hierarchy of Horrors was monitored, measured, reported and reacted to quickly. When performance standards were not met, the specific employee, station or department was identified, held accountable and was responsible for rapid improvement. There were no secrets as to how the local FedEx team was doing. The information was posted every day and everyone's performance reviews and raises were tied to the Hierarchy of Horrors.

The result? A year after introducing the Hierarchy of Horrors, service failures were down 11 percent while package volume was up 20 percent. Several years later, FedEx was the first service organization to win the prestigious Malcolm Baldrige National Quality Award. There are many factors that go into winning the award, but I believe FedEx won because their team was connected to a common goal, understood what was REALLY important and knew the score every day. FedEx won because they knew precisely what it took to win.

Q: Are you keeping score?

A: 1. Clearly define the results you expect from your team.

2. Brainstorm every situation that could prevent your team from achieving those results — these are your "horrors."

3. For each of your "horrors," develop a plan to attack it with preventative measures so you can ensure it does not happen to your team.

4. Measure what matters and monitor your results daily.

5. Provide accurate and immediate feedback so that your team can make the adjustments necessary to win.

6. Celebrate your wins!

HUDDLE UP

As your team's GPS, it is crucial that you monitor results and provide timely feedback to the team. Your car's GPS is constantly monitoring your progress. If it only checked your location every 20 miles, you could be way off course and not know it.

Likewise, a football coach doesn't wait until halftime to check the score and give his team feedback. He assesses the outcome of every single play and adjusts accordingly. If the play goes as planned, he recognizes people for playing their positions well and working together as a team. If the play doesn't produce the results he was expecting, the team huddles up, figures out what went wrong and makes adjustments, and the coach works with individuals as necessary for improved performance.

When you huddle up and listen up, you have a better chance of not messing up. If your team knows the score, they better understand the need for adjustments and are more open to change. They will also be more receptive to coaching and constructive feedback. Answer the question, "How is our team doing?" and the team will be energized to do what is necessary to win.

Fortune magazine has recognized The Container Store as one of the Top 100 Best Companies to Work for in America for 12 consecutive years. Twelve years…think of the changes that have happened in the world over the past 12 years. Yet, through it all, The Container Store has maintained its leadership position in the retail industry. One major reason why it is a great place to work is because one of their guiding principles is that communication is leadership. Every day each store has "huddles" to share information about what is going on within their store and within the entire organization. During the day, they may call emergency huddles to re-focus on that particular day's activities.

Another successful organization is Ritz-Carlton, one of the best known hotel chains in the world. One reason that Ritz-Carlton is consistently among the highest-rated hotels is because of the way they communicate with their employees. They operate with an "Open Kimono" management philosophy – everything is shared with team members.

Before every shift, teams meet for 10 minutes to review critical information. Each employee receives a small packet with the day's vital information: projected hotel occupancy; a list of VIP guests and their preferences; special conference/meeting needs; and a motivational principle of the day. These huddles ensure that everyone knows what is REALLY important and how their performance impacts customer satisfaction. Everyone is on the same page every day.

A retail store and a high-end hotel chain share the same philosophy that winning involves telling the team how they are doing. They both "huddle up" and share critical information. That is not by accident; it is intentional. They know that the more informed people are, the better they will perform.

Ask Yourself...

How is the team doing?

Are you creating a positive environment for your team? Are people smiling, showing up on time and proactively taking care of their customers? You control the thermostat that sets the "climate" for your team.

TEAMWORK IS CONNECTED INDEPENDENCE

You've probably worked with some great (and not so great) leaders. One person whom I learned a lot from was the least effective leader I've ever seen. His method of leadership was to pit the teams within his organization against each other – sales was bad for operations, operations was bad for sales, finance was the enemy to all. Needless to say, there was no sense of teamwork. He said and did whatever was on his mind at the time without considering the impact. It sounds crazy, but that was the way he led. And he did lead his company…straight into bankruptcy!

I call his leadership philosophy Tumbleweed Leadership. If you've ever been to a dry, arid climate like Arizona, you've probably seen tumbleweeds all over the place…blowing here and there, in all different directions. A tumbleweed is an above-ground plant that, once mature and dry, disengages from the root and tumbles away in the wind. It has no control over where it goes – the wind is in charge.

Tumbleweed Leadership will destroy your team and your organization. Without the roots of respect, trust, accountability, teamwork and commonly shared goals, your team members will tumble here and there, with no sense of direction other than where the wind pushes them that particular day.

In contrast, winning leadership is like a redwood tree. Have you ever seen a magnificent redwood tree? Growing over 300 feet tall – higher than the length of three football fields – they tower above all other trees. Most of them have scars on their trunks reflecting tough times; some even have huge caverns carved through their trunks by wildfire. But still they grow. Redwoods are so full of life, it's difficult to kill one.

The secret to the redwood's amazing ability to survive and endure is not in the tree itself. Redwoods grow in clusters. Their strength is their root system, but not a typical root system that is independent and grows downward. You might think that redwoods are able to grow so tall because of their deep roots; but in fact, they have no tap root and their roots may reach no deeper than 6 to 12 feet. For every foot in height, the redwood tree sends its roots three times that distance…not down, but out! If the tree is 300 feet tall, its roots go out 900 feet, intertwining with the roots from the other redwoods in the grove.

Redwoods can withstand the elements and even the ravages of fire because they are connected. The roots in a grove are so interwoven that it's impossible to tell which roots belong to which tree. Standing alone, an individual redwood could easily fall; but intertwined and standing together, they strengthen and support each other. Each tree is independent, but they are connected through their roots by a common goal – survival.

Leaders who connect and intertwine their team members through commonly shared values and goals practice what I call Redwood Leadership. These leaders consistently reinforce what is REALLY important, place great emphasis on teamwork and constantly let their teams know how they are doing. These are the roots that hold the team together. Team members are aligned, support each other and are accountable to one another. If you study high-performing teams, you will find that they are Redwood Teams.

Umbra, a leader in innovative and affordable items for the home, practices Redwood Leadership. Their website notes: "Teamwork is the foundation of our company culture. We encourage everyone to help our customers by first helping each other. The 'it's not my job' mentality does not exist at Umbra. Our employees share a collective entrepreneurial attitude that keeps Umbra a leader in the design industry." Leaders hold weekly meetings with the entire organization – founders, engineers, designers, salespeople and sometimes customers. They discuss every product in the development process and make a decision to proceed, kill the idea or change it. No matter their department or position, team members' roots are intertwined.

There is a stark contrast between Tumbleweed Leadership and Redwood Leadership. The tumbleweed is dried up and dead; it goes wherever the winds take it. The redwood is strong…always growing higher…connected to all the other trees in the grove. When you link your team together with shared goals and shared knowledge, they will be able to withstand the tough times that will inevitably come their way.

Q: Do you have a Tumbleweed Team or a Redwood Team?

A: During your next team meeting, provide everyone with a blank sheet of paper and ask them to chart the workflow through your team. From the point the "system" begins to the point it is completed, what happens? Who does what? What impact does each person have on the rest of the team? What happens if one person is a tumbleweed?

You may be surprised at the different answers you receive. One discovery that your team will definitely make is that it needs to be intertwined like the redwood. You cannot expect great, long-lasting results with team members who are only interested in their personal results.

TUMBLEWEEDS IN THE REDWOOD GROVE

Even Redwood Leaders occasionally have to deal with tumbleweeds – people who insist on going their own direction without regard to the rest of the team. Every organization has problem employees. Tumbleweed people may be uncooperative, chronically late or negative and cynical. Or perhaps they do just enough to get by. Although problem employees represent a small percentage of your team, they take up a disproportionate amount of your time, energy and enthusiasm – all of which could be used in more constructive ways.

If you have a tumbleweed on your team, you may think that you have failed as a leader, but that is not necessarily true. You can't fix everyone's weaknesses, and not every person has unlimited potential. Your job is to guide and coach team members, but it is their responsibility to grow in the redwood grove as opposed to being a loose tumbleweed. As the leader, you can influence that decision but you can't control it. What you can control is how you address the issue.

If you ignore the tumbleweed, it will continue on its own, blowing in the wind. But allowing problem employees to "skate by" only reinforces their commonly held belief that the less they do, the less they'll be asked to do. And since your team's workload is not likely to decrease, you might be inclined to spread the work out to the rest of the team. This is not a good strategy!

Ignoring tumbleweeds has a huge, detrimental impact on your entire team. You cannot be successful in the long term without addressing performance issues. I assure you that any issue you ignore will not go unnoticed by your team. If you do not hold tumbleweeds accountable, you will lose credibility with the rest of your team. They are always watching you and will remember how you handle tumbleweeds or any other obstacles that prevent the team from winning.

If your tumbleweeds are not interested in working with the rest of the team, there might be a deeper issue. Why don't they care? Perhaps in the past they didn't know what was REALLY important or how they were doing. If that is the case, good coaching should take care of the issue.

As you prepare to coach the tumbleweed, go through this checklist to make sure you are doing everything possible to provide them with the opportunity to succeed:

1. Are your expectations crystal clear? How do you know?

2. Are your expectations reasonable and fair? How do you know?

3. Has the team member received adequate training to do the job properly? How do you know?

4. Do they understand why it is important to do the job properly? How do you know?

5. Are you holding them accountable for their performance? Are there appropriate and consistent consequences for non-performance? How do you know?

6. Do you consistently recognize and reward positive performance? How do you know?

7. Have you given them the freedom to be successful? How do you know?

8. Have performance obstacles been removed? How do you know?

If you answered "yes" to each question above, you have done all you can do, and now it is up to the tumbleweed to change. But what if they choose not to? Then roll up your sleeves, because that is when the toughest job of a leader begins.

Each team works within a clearly stated set of boundaries. If the tumbleweed chooses to operate outside the boundaries, they in effect have chosen to tumble somewhere else, and you have to implement their decision. Certainly it is difficult to watch people leave, but it is far worse for your team if you allow them to stay.

Addressing performance problems is tough, stressful and draining, but you must dig down and find the courage to confront the issue. Remember that there are resources available to help you. Call in Human Resources – they are the experts. There are also great books dedicated solely to the subject of coaching, including *The Manager's Coaching Handbook,* which will guide you through the exact steps of coaching your tumbleweed to improve.

Your tumbleweeds may choose to become redwoods, or they may decide to tumble away – it is their choice. Either way, you win.

COMMON GOALS ARE NOT THE SAME AS COMMON INTERESTS

While it is crucial that every member of your team work together toward a common goal, it is not necessary for everyone on your team to have common interests or to like each other outside of the office. Likeability is not nearly as important as mutual respect. It's possible that your team's culture might be more pleasant if everyone was alike, but people are different. It is that diversity, in fact, that often drives creativity and innovation.

I am a huge college football fan, and I enjoy going to the games and cheering my team (the University of Arkansas Razorbacks) to victory. Sitting in the stadium, I am with a group of people who may have nothing else in common other than loving the Razorbacks. We are of all ages, sizes, socioeconomic levels, nationalities and political persuasions. Yet, for a few hours on Saturday afternoons in the Fall, we are all Razorback fans, and we want our team to win. When there is a bad call against our team, we let the referee know. When our team scores, we celebrate. When we win, we party. When we lose, we share the loss together. And when the game ends, we go our separate ways.

I think this is similar to the relationships with teammates at work. You don't have to have a lot in common with each other, except that you are committed to the same goals every day at work. You can all be independent and yet still connected, still a team.

Answer the Third Question:
How is our team doing?

○ Everyone wants to know if their team is winning.

○ The more knowledge you share about how all of the pieces work together, the more confidence and power you give your team.

○ Know the score – measure what matters and monitor it on a regular basis. Celebrate when the team is achieving its objectives.

○ Understand your Hierarchy of Horrors and put a plan together to make sure that the horrors do not happen.

○ When you huddle up and listen up, you have a better chance of not messing up.

○ Tumbleweed Leadership will destroy your team. Redwood Leadership will help your team work together to withstand the challenges they will face.

○ Redwood Leaders connect and intertwine their team members through commonly shared values and goals.

○ If you have tumbleweeds on your team, don't ignore them. Coach them to improve or help them tumble someplace else.

When you answer the question,
"How is our team doing?"
you create a positive, winning atmosphere.

The Fourth Question

Do you care?

*"Nobody cares how much you know,
until they know how much you care."*

— Theodore Roosevelt

Recently, I was sitting in an airport when I overheard two people talking. The subject was their boss – no big surprise there. Both of them said they liked the boss, but one said, "She never returns my calls. She only calls me when it fits her agenda. That drives me crazy." The other person agreed and then added, "I don't think she really cares."

Both of these people may stay with their organization for a long time, but I wouldn't bet on it.

Oftentimes leaders get so focused on the "big things" that they forget to take care of the basics, like showing the people on their team that they sincerely care about them. As the poet Robert W.

Service said, "It isn't the mountain ahead that wears you out; it's the grain of sand in your shoe." Many times the "grain of sand" that keeps a team from achieving its goals is lack of attention or respect from their leader.

Every person on your team has the need to be understood, accepted and appreciated. Their unspoken question is, "Do you care?" What they mean is, do you care about them as a person...as more than just another cog in the company wheel?

You are already answering that question, whether you know it or not. Even if you are not consciously and verbally answering the question, it is always being answered by your actions. Of course, it is never your intent to create an environment where your team assumes you don't care about them, but that may be the signal you're sending nonetheless. Perhaps that is why you are surprised when an unexpected resignation hits your desk.

When people are in the midst of uncertainty, are overworked, feel they are carrying a disproportionate share of the load, or believe they are being mistreated, they immediately assume you do not care. That isn't fair, but that's just the way it is. Even Jesus' disciples questioned whether he cared about them. His disciples had seen Him perform miracle after miracle. Yet when they found themselves in a boat during a raging storm, they woke Jesus and asked, "Teacher, don't you care?" After all the times they saw Him take care of others, when they were uncertain and fearful, they still questioned if He cared about them.

If Jesus had to answer this question, think how much more often you have to answer the same question for your team. When was the last time your team saw you performing miracles? It doesn't really matter how much your team sees you showing others –

such as customers – that you care. Every individual on the team needs to know that you care about them personally.

WHAT ABOUT MONEY?

If you believe the typical exit interview, great people leave good organizations to start over someplace else because of money or advancement opportunities. But don't believe those exit interviews! After all, the person leaving your organization doesn't want to burn any bridges and has nothing to gain by telling the whole truth. So they choose the path of least resistance.

Occasionally, the difference in money is significant enough to warrant a move, but most of the time it's not about money or career advancement. In a recent survey,[6] 89 percent of managers stated that they believed employees leave because of money. Yet in a parallel survey of employees who left organizations, 88 percent of people said they left for reasons not related to money. Let those statistics sink in…only 12 percent of people left because of money.

Now consider the situation from the other side: When you interview someone for a position and ask why they are thinking about leaving their current job, what do they say? Most do not say, "Because you are going to pay me more." In fact, I can't remember ever hearing anyone say that. The most common response is something like, "Because my efforts and contributions aren't appreciated where I'm currently working." If people on your team are interviewing with other organizations, that is probably the same answer they are giving in their interviews.

The real reason that great people leave good organizations is simply this: their needs for respect, appreciation, training and recognition

---

[6] By the Saratoga Institute

are not being met. Their perception is that they work hard, do the right things and yet nobody cares. People need more than pay and benefits. They need to know that you care about them and that their contributions are appreciated. The truth is that people leave *people* long before they leave organizations. They give up hope that their leader will ever meet their needs and conclude that the unknown leader will be better than the known.

Assuming that your compensation package is competitive, if you are looking for the paycheck to answer the question of whether you care, you will be sorely disappointed with the results. Even a raise in pay is only a short-term boost at best. Money is the most expensive and least efficient way you can show you care.

INVEST YOUR TIME AND ATTENTION

Conversely, the least expensive and most effective way to show you care is to invest your time and attention with your people. And the more you invest, the greater your return will be. One of your top priorities as a leader is to be available for your team. If you are always busy in "management land," you send the signal that everything else is more important than your team. Spend your time just drilling down into the numbers, and they will assume you only care about the numbers. That is a bad signal to send to the people you need to perform in order for you to be successful.

"Do you care?" is a personal question asked by *individuals* on your team. That means you must answer the question individually. You must give your time and attention to what is important to each of them, not what is important to you or to their teammates. Of course, you can count on family, success and job satisfaction being important to all of them. Invest your time and attention on these areas, and they will know that you care.

But rewards and recognition should be personalized. It doesn't do you any good to reward someone with something that is important to you but that they do not care about. In fact, it may do more harm than good. I learned this the hard way a few years ago when I "rewarded" one of my top performers with my 30-yard line tickets to a conference championship football game. Those tickets were extremely important to me, but the game was the same day as my daughter's wedding, and obviously I wasn't going to miss the wedding. So I created a contest for my team, and the winner got my tickets to the game.

The person who won the contest was not a football fan. As unbelievable as it was to me, he didn't even know about the conference championship. He went to the game, but it didn't mean much to him. I later found out he was a movie buff, and he would have been happier if I'd given him tickets to a movie. It would have cost me a lot less; but more importantly, it would have been more meaningful to him, and he would have had a lot more fun.

The lesson? Recognition is in the eye of the beholder. If you want to show you care, demonstrate it with things that are important to the individual. Recognition doesn't have to be formal, and it doesn't have to necessarily be a big deal. It simply requires your focus and attention.

Q: How does my team know I care?

A: Answer TRUE or FALSE to the following statements to determine if you are showing your team that you care:

1. I hire great people.

2. I de-hire those who do not carry their share of the load.

3. My meetings are productive, on-time and last only as long as necessary.

4. I recognize positive performance immediately.

5. We celebrate victories together.

BUILD RELATIONSHIPS

We are connected today as we've never been before. We are texted, emailed, blogged, instant-messaged, LinkedIn, Facebooked, Twittered, mapped, GPSed, web-enabled, Blackberried, iPhoned and Googled with real-time information and news. Earth-orbiting satellites know where we are every second, how many inches we are from our favorite restaurant and whether our air bags have deployed. We are connected to technology, but not necessarily to one another.

Technology has been a great productivity enhancement tool for many aspects of leadership, but it can be a detriment to maintaining personal relationships with your team members. It may seem counterintuitive, but the more you use technology in your communications, the more face-to-face contact you need to have with your team.

You cannot demonstrate that you care electronically. You must build personal relationships with your people. Answering the basic human-relations question, "Do you care?," involves a one-on-one expression in person. A handshake and a look in the eyes to say, "Thank you" have a far greater impact than any message on a screen.

Here are some simple yet effective ways to build relationships with your team and show you care:

1. Practice forgiveness and ask for forgiveness. No one is perfect – even you – and there will come a time when you need to ask your team for forgiveness. When you forgive others, they are more likely to forgive you in return.

2. Treat everyone with respect and dignity. Even if you disagree, you can disagree respectfully.

3. A team member's personal crisis is your test as a leader who cares. How will you respond? If you are encouraging, empathic and helpful, you will pass the test. If you ignore the situation, act disinterested or lose control, your answer is clear as well.

4. Write personal notes. It may sound old-school, but a personal, handwritten note sent to their home will mean more to your team members than any email, text or memo you could send.

5. Small things matter. Chip Conley, author of *Peak* and owner of several successful boutique hotels, has given away hundreds of copies of the children's book *The Little Engine That Could* to his employees as appreciation for their can-do attitude. The book could have been purchased for a few dollars by any person on his team, but it wouldn't have had the same meaning. The real value of this gift was that Chip cared

enough to include a personal, handwritten note to each team member and handed out the books himself. That little book was a powerful form of recognition for his team.

LISTEN

A popular television reality show is "Undercover Boss." I enjoy the show, but it disturbs me at the same time. Why does the CEO have to disguise himself and go to the front line to find out what is really going on in his organization? Why is he surprised to find out that some of the corporate programs are actually punishing people for doing their job? Why is he surprised to discover that people's needs are not being met? Why are decisions being made without anyone representing the front line?

Perhaps because leaders aren't listening.

Many team members wonder, "Why do we shoot ourselves in the foot? If leadership would only ask us before they made decisions, we could then save a lot of re-work, mistakes, conflicts and money." They are usually right.

As a leader, you do not need to have all the answers. No one has all the answers. But in most cases, your team has the answers to the challenges you're facing. They know how to solve most organizational problems – you just need to ask them. The best answers come from the people on the front line. They are in the best position to make decisions affecting them.

When you allow your team to have input on issues and you listen with the intent to act on their suggestions, you create positive energy. Involvement in the decision-making process is one of the greatest motivators for your people. And the more you involve them, the more they will buy into what your team is trying to accomplish.

It is up to you to create an environment in which they can freely share their thoughts and ideas, and then to listen with an open mind. Sam Walton once said, "I know what I know; I want to know what you know." Another highly successful leader, hotel mogul Bill Marriott, believes the seven most important words a leader can say are: "I don't know...what do you think?"

The J.M. Smucker Company (as in Smucker's jellies and jams) is consistently cited by *Fortune* magazine as one of the best 100 companies in America to work for. Their "secret" is to continue to do what they have done for many years – live by a very simple code of conduct. That code is to listen with your full attention, to look for the good in others, to have a sense of humor (but not at the expense of others) and to say thank you for a job well done. Isn't it interesting that listening is the first and most important item on the list? Without listening to their people, the remaining code of conduct would be worthless.

When you listen to your team and act on their suggestions, not only are you more likely to get the best outcome, but you also show that you care. Even if your team's idea is not feasible to implement, if you appreciate their input and let them know why it's not feasible, you will answer their question, "Do you care?"

As you seek to listen and to gather input from the people in your organization, remember that the higher you are in the organization, the tougher it is to discover the truth (but that is no excuse for trying). Everyone in between the front line and the top line filters information, so oftentimes neither the front line nor the top line gets the full story. As a result, many decisions are made that drive the front line crazy, and the poor implementation of those decisions drives the top line crazy. Then everyone is asking, "Why doesn't anybody around here care?"

RESPECT THEIR TIME

Meetings are an unavoidable necessity, but they are also one of the biggest wastes of people's time. If your team is constantly tied up in long, unproductive meetings, they will begin to think that you don't respect their time.

Here's a scary statistic – the average person wastes about 250 hours per year in unproductive meetings. Another alarming fact: Meetings are expensive, probably the largest expense that doesn't have a line item on the income statement. Think about it…a one-hour meeting of a dozen executives could easily cost $5,000 or more. That's a lot of time and money being wasted!

Yet when everyone is prepared, on time and focused, most meetings can be accomplished in half the time. The best way to get your team onboard (and show your team that you care) is to ask them for suggestions and allow them to take ownership of making your meetings better. This gives them a stake in the process and motivates them to keep your meetings productive.

Here are some additional ideas for making your meetings productive but short:

- **Make sure every meeting is absolutely necessary**. Don't fall into the "perpetually scheduled meeting syndrome," in which you have meetings just because meetings are regularly scheduled. Routine meetings are not a good investment unless they help you accomplish your objectives.

- **Have a set agenda and always cover the most important items first.** That way you ensure that you cover what you need to accomplish, and you're not rushing through the important items at the end. If you're spending thousands of dollars on a meeting, it is probably not a good investment to start by solving a $100 problem. Instead, start with the most important items and work your way down to the least important. The last item on the agenda – and the one you always want to cover before the end of the meeting – should be a recap of the decisions made during the meeting along with who is responsible for which tasks going forward.

○ **Start your meetings on time.** It's a bad investment to start a meeting later than scheduled. Think about this: You waste 30 minutes of productivity by beginning a meeting with 10 people just three minutes late. Avoid the temptation of recapping what has happened when someone shows up late. Not only does that reward the tardy person, it's also disrespectful to the people who were on time. There should be accountability with your meetings with a penalty for showing up late. Reward the people who made it on time with a well-planned, productive session.

○ **Don't allow people to continue to "sell" their points after a decision has been made.** Some people like to fight losing battles. Don't fall for that. Set limits on the time allowed per item and move forward.

○ **End your meetings on time.** If your meeting is scheduled to end at 3:00 p.m., everyone will begin looking at their watches the minute you hit 3:01, wondering how much longer the meeting will last. You can rest assured that your productivity goes out the window when the scheduled meeting time has passed.

SURROUND YOUR GREAT PEOPLE WITH OTHER GREAT PEOPLE

Choosing who will be part of your team is the most important single decision you make as a leader. One great hire is better and more productive than two or three average hires. If you hire the best people, effectively train them and get out of their way, you don't have to hire very many. Having great people on the team is a better investment, less stressful and more enjoyable for you and your team. And being around great people makes you better!

Answer the question, "Do you care?" by only hiring great, qualified candidates who enhance the team. It is your job to continually upgrade your team. If you lower your standards just to fill a position, you demonstrate that you don't really care about your team at all. Never settle for someone who may have the potential to be good but who you know down deep will probably never be great. You will pay for that decision later. Remember, what you see in the interview is the best that candidates have to offer – and it's not going to get better.

Another way to demonstrate that you care is to actively involve your team in the hiring process. After all, the new person will have an impact on everyone – positively or negatively. Why not include your team in the selection process? People support what they help create, and you give them a precious gift – respect and trust – by allowing them to be involved.

One of the most successful businesses in a very competitive environment is Whole Foods Market, a natural and organic food retailer. Their philosophy is to let the whole team hire. That makes good sense – the person hired feels an obligation to the entire team, but more importantly, every person on the team feels an obligation to make a successful selection.

Here are a few tips to help you find the right people for your team and engage your team in the hiring process:

○ Clearly and accurately define in writing the skills and attributes the perfect candidate will bring to your organization. Then create an interview outline to ensure you ask each candidate the same questions in the same order. This allows you to concentrate on the candidates' responses and evaluate what they say, rather than worrying about what your next question will be.

○ Actively search for candidates who have different skills and qualities than you and your current team members. Sociological studies show that most leaders hire people just like themselves. But this limits the opportunity to build a diverse group of individuals who bring a variety of skills and talents to the table and are therefore better able to deliver results.

○ Your best source for candidates is recommendations from your current top performers. They know the job and the culture and will have a good feel for whether the candidate has the necessary skills to be an outstanding contributor and will be a good fit with your culture.

○ When interviewing candidates, use the 3 Rules of 3:

1. Interview at least 3 qualified candidates for each position;

2. Interview each candidate at least 3 times; and

3. Have at least 3 team members evaluate each candidate.

○ Interview candidates at different times during the day, for example, in the early morning the first time and in the afternoon another time. You're hiring them to work all day long; it might be wise to see how they perform at different times of the day.

○ When evaluating candidates, consider talent and "fit" equally. The most talented person may not be the best choice if they don't fit with the talent that already exists on your team.

○ Seek the help of your Human Resources department for legal issues, interviewing tips, interview questions, etc. There are also numerous books available on the subject of interviewing skills and techniques. Successful leaders don't necessarily need to have excellent interviewing skills – they just need to know where to go for help when the time comes.

Take your time and find the best person, not just the best person available. Look for people who exceed your requirements and are hungry for knowledge and success. If you are stretching someone's ability in order to fill your pressing need, you are making a mistake that will negatively impact the new person, you and your team. Instead, hire SWANs: Smart people who Work hard, are Ambitious and are Nice.

Ask *Yourself*...

Do they know I care?

What did you do today to show you care? Did you seek opportunities to communicate one-on-one? Did you eliminate obstacles for your team? Were you available for them?

Answer the Fourth Question:
Do you care?

○ Everyone on your team has a need to be understood, accepted and appreciated – to know that you care about them as a person.

○ People leave people more often than they leave organizations. Rarely do they leave because of money.

○ Money is the most expensive and least efficient way you can show you care.

○ The best way to show you care is to invest your time and attention with your team. Don't be so focused on things in "management land" that you forget to take care of your people.

○ Recognize individual team members in a way that is personalized and meaningful to them.

○ You cannot depend on technology to broadcast the message that you care. You must build relationships face-to-face with your people.

○ Ask team members for their input on important decisions, listen to them with an open mind, and act on their suggestions whenever possible.

○ Respect your team's time by holding only highly productive meetings that are as short as possible.

○ Prove to your team that you care by only hiring truly qualified candidates who will make the team better, and be sure to include the team in the hiring process.

When you answer the question,
"Do you care?"
your team will reward you with their loyalty.

THE FIFTH QUESTION

What difference do we make?

"People want to work for a cause, not just for a living."
– C. WILLIAM POLLARD, *The Soul of the Firm*

You may think that airline baggage handlers have a pretty thankless job – load heavy bags on planes at all times of the day and night, all year-round in the extreme heat and cold, even on weekends and holidays…and never see a customer who thanks them for what they do. I think it would be difficult for most people to be passionate about being a baggage handler.

But I recently came across a story[7] about one particular Southwest Airlines baggage handler who was passionate about his job. This man had a wife and three children at home. When his kids began to complain about Daddy working on Thanksgiving again, he gathered them around and told them: "If Daddy didn't go to

---

[7] As told in *It's Not What You Sell, It's What You Stand For*, Roy Spence, Portfolio, 2009

work, many families wouldn't be able to fly around the country and be with their loved ones. Without Daddy doing his job, little kids all across the country wouldn't get to see their grandparents, their aunts and uncles, or any of their cousins. Daddy has to go to work to make sure everyone can be with their families."

This baggage handler got it! He understood that his job was not loading luggage – he was making other people's lives better. He clearly knew the answer to the fifth question: "What difference do we make?" Once their basic needs are met, people need to know that they are making a positive difference. William James summed it up brilliantly: "Act as if what you do makes a difference. It does."

The previous four questions focused on team dynamics. Once those questions are answered, your team will turn their attention to organizational dynamics. The fifth question, "What difference do we make?," is irrelevant if you haven't answered the first four. If you have, your team will next want to understand the role they play in the organization's purpose.

Research consistently shows that belief and involvement in the organization's mission is one of the factors people consider most important in a job. When your team clearly understands the difference they make with customers, in your community or in the world, it can completely change their attitude about their job. People who think they are part of a larger purpose or cause are energized and engaged.

On the other hand, if you want to demoralize your team, have them spend their time doing pointless tasks that serve no greater purpose. The Nazis demonstrated this by forcing many of their prisoners to dig a hole, then fill it back in. Day after day – dig and fill, dig and fill, dig and fill. The Nazi camp doctors discovered that the prisoners doing the pointless work of digging and filling died more quickly than those who were given meaningful chores.

Your team is no different – they will become disengaged if they must do things they perceive as pointless and serve no greater purpose or when they don't see how their work fits into the bigger picture. They want to know that what they are doing is REALLY important and part of a meaningful mission.

Being Connected to a Greater Cause Creates Passion

Passionate people are the fuel that drives your organization and gives it a competitive advantage. Even in the most difficult times, passionate people will figure out a way to get things done. And when your people are passionate about their job and the organization's purpose, they will naturally share their passion with others. They become positive evangelists for your organization.

Zappos – the online shoe and apparel retailer – is an organization that knows how to create passionate employees. I recently visited the Zappos headquarters near Las Vegas. I took the tour that is available to the public, and no one knew who I was or why I was there. My mission was to find out what is so special about Zappos that it is consistently recognized as one of the top companies in America to work for and one of the Top 50 Most Engaged Organizations.

According to their website, Zappos says this about their purpose:

> *We've aligned the entire organization around one mission: to provide the best customer service possible. Internally, we call this our WOW philosophy. At Zappos, anything worth doing is worth doing with WOW.*

> *To WOW, you must differentiate yourself, which means doing something a little unconventional and innovative. You must do*

something that's above and beyond what's expected. And whatever you do must have an emotional impact on the receiver. We are not an average company, our service is not average, and we don't want our people to be average. We expect every employee to deliver WOW.

Whether internally with co-workers or externally with our customers and partners, delivering WOW results in word of mouth. Our philosophy at Zappos is to WOW with service and experience, not with anything that relates directly to monetary compensation (for example, we don't offer blanket discounts or promotions to customers). We seek to WOW our customers, our co-workers, our vendors, our partners, and in the long run, our investors.

It didn't take long to see this WOW philosophy in action. A Zappos employee named Zack picked me up at my hotel in a Zappos van. During the 15-minute trip back to the company, Zack filled me in on the Zappos culture and why he loves to work there. His main point of emphasis: "We are a team." (Randy, my driver back to the hotel at the end of the tour, was also an informed, enthusiastic salesman and representative for Zappos.)

Walking into the headquarters building, I immediately noticed the energy, excitement, fun and "a little weirdness," as Zappos team members call it. My tour guide was Rocco, and he was both passionate and entertaining. The highlight of the tour was Zappos' call center, known as the Customer Loyalty Team ("CLT"). This is where new team members quickly discover how Zappos delivers WOW to their customers. Every new employee – regardless of position, title or pay – begins with four weeks of training with the CLT. Even accountants and corporate attorneys spend their first four weeks on the CLT. Permanent members of the Customer Loyalty

Team start fresh every six months by changing their physical location and management. By the way, employee turnover in the CLT is around 6 percent, far less than in a typical call center environment.

Interestingly, none of the Zappos team members I met ever mentioned upper management. Instead, they talked about the company's core values. I didn't learn anything about top leadership until the tour got to their cubicle area. It was decorated like a jungle and called Monkey Row, and it reflected what I had seen all day – fun, enthusiasm and a little weirdness. The CEO was front and center. There was no such thing as an open-door policy on Monkey Row – it's difficult to have an open-door policy if you have no doors.

A culture like Zappos' won't necessarily work at every organization. But Zappos does something that you and every leader in every organization can learn from: They constantly and passionately preach their mission of WOW and engage each employee in becoming a part of that mission. Every single team member is committed to delivering WOW, no matter their job. I experienced that WOW firsthand.

You can foster passionate people just like Zappos does by clearly and directly tying their everyday work to the purpose of the organization. When I was at FedEx, our people "bled purple." We loved what we were doing and the difference we were making in the world, one package at a time. The passionate people who serve in our armed forces are driven by their purpose – to protect our freedom. Go into a Whole Foods Market, and you'll be helped by someone who is passionate about changing the eating habits of America. At The Container Store, you will find people who are passionate about organizing your life. Mary Kay is in the business of making people feel good. Disney makes dreams come true. Google makes the world's information universally accessible and useful. The person behind the counter at Chick-fil-A is passionate about making your dining experience in a fast-food restaurant as enjoyable as it is affordable.

Passion is not something that you can turn on like a light switch. You can't fake it or force it upon people. The key to creating a team of passionate people is for each person to clearly understand that they make a difference in the world, over and above just doing their job.

WHAT DOES YOUR ORGANIZATION REALLY STAND FOR?

Does your team know what your organization stands for...what it REALLY stands for? Almost every organization has published values that are composed of nice, well-thought-out words. But those words are meaningless unless everyone in the organization, from the top to the bottom, totally commits to them and walks the talk. The mission, vision and values that you put on paper are only worth the cost of the paper; your actions are what counts.

Even Enron, one of the most corrupt companies of the last century, had great-sounding values. Enron's values of Respect, Integrity, Communication and Excellence could be found on plaques on the walls, on screen savers and in annual reports. They were talked about in meetings. Those values sounded great at the time, but they sound sort of silly now. Enron probably spent hundreds of hours and thousands of dollars identifying which values to list. But the values didn't mean anything – the way they ran their company meant everything.

I'd be willing to bet that the major U.S. airlines talk a good game when it comes to their values. They probably have values about serving the customer, taking care of employees and the like. I'd also be willing to bet that these organizations believe in their values. Yet most of these same airlines have instituted of new practice of charging passengers for checked baggage.

How has this new rule played out? Customers are not happy because they have to cram everything into a small suitcase or pay a significant sum of money to check a bag roundtrip. The flight attendants are upset because they are now baggage handlers. The curbside baggage handlers are disappointed because fewer people are checking bags and those who do are less inclined to tip. The pilots are angry because it takes longer to get all the carry-on baggage stored properly, jeopardizing their critical on-time departure.

So what do most people think these companies stand for? Profit! That may not be true, but that's the perception. Their actions speak louder than their words. Is it worth upsetting customers, flight attendants, baggage handlers, pilots and everyone else to make an extra $30 per person? Do you think the employees of these companies believe they are making a positive difference in the lives of others?

It doesn't matter what you say as an organization; what matters is what you do. If you are not living up to your stated values, you are clearly sending a message to employees about what your organization really stands for…but it's probably not the kind of message you were hoping for.

SHARED KNOWLEDGE CREATES POSITIVE ENERGY
Sharing knowledge and teaching employees the business of the business helps them understand their impact on the organization and its purpose. The more information you share about the "why" behind the "what" you are trying to accomplish, the better your team members will see the organizational vision and support the strategies necessary to achieve that vision. Peter Drucker, one of

the greatest leadership gurus of all time, once said that everyone in an organization should know the answer to these two questions: "What is our business?" and "How is business?"

There is no good reason that anyone should be left in the dark about how all of the pieces of the organization fit together. Every team and department should clearly understand how they are connected to and affected by every other team and department. However, most organizations inadvertently operate under the "95/5 Rule." The 95/5 Rule is based on the reality that most work groups understand about 95 percent of what goes on in their own department. There may be a few things that happen that are a mystery, but by and large, they know what is going on within their team.

The "5" of the 95/5 Rule represents the percentage that a typical team knows about other departments and teams within the organization. Only 5 percent? Shouldn't they know more about other parts of the organization? Wouldn't things work better if the team understood the big picture? Isn't it reasonable for your team to know how all of the pieces fit together? The answer to all of these questions is, of course, yes.

The more knowledge your team has, the better decisions they will make and the greater their positive impact on other work groups. You will also discover that changing the 95/5 Rule to a more informed 95/25 Rule (or even more) will increase productivity, save time and improve everyone's morale.

If you can tear down the walls between teams and demonstrate how each one plays an important role in the larger cause, they will begin to support each other. When your team understands the impact they have on the entire organization, suddenly they will begin to look at things differently. They may discover that while their team is "winning," they are causing another team in the organization to "lose." That is why answering the question, "What difference do we make?," is so important. Your team is not an island. Everything they do impacts the rest of the organization.

Ask *Yourself...*

Have I reminded my team of their purpose?

How many times today did you reinforce the impact your team makes on your customers and the rest of the organization??

YOU MAKE A DIFFERENCE

Many leaders underestimate the difference that their team can make within the organization. It is hard to know up front the impact you can make. To illustrate how a small change can make a huge difference, let's take a look at the Butterfly Effect – a discovery made by meteorologist Edward Lorenz.

Lorenz used computer simulation to track and model weather patterns. He entered data on wind speed, air pressure and temperature into three linked equations. The calculations formed a mathematical loop – the results of the first equation were fed into the second, the results of which were fed into the third equation, and the output of the third equation was ultimately the input back into the first equation. By using the mathematical loop calculations, Lorenz found he could predict weather with some accuracy.

Most mathematicians check and re-check their calculations, and Lorenz was no exception. One day while rechecking the results of his complex weather calculations, Lorenz took a shortcut: he entered the same data he'd used previously except he rounded each number to the nearest one thousandth rather than to the nearest one millionth. (For example, 0.506 instead of 0.506127.)

You'd think that this minor adjustment in the data would have only a minor impact on the overall results, perhaps no more than one-tenth of 1 percent, right? Yet when Lorenz examined the results, he was amazed to discover a significant difference in the two calculations. The infinitesimal change he made in the input was magnified by the feedback process in the mathematical loop, and the results were greatly altered. This discovery ultimately led the meteorologist to wonder, "Does the flap of a butterfly's wings in Brazil cause a tornado in Texas?"

Since then, the Butterfly Effect has become a familiar illustration to describe how a small change in a dynamic system can cause a chain of events that leads to large-scale difference. Enterprise Rent-A-Car is a great example of how the Butterfly Effect can work in business. Several years ago, an Enterprise employee in Florida suggested that Enterprise pick up customers instead of asking them to wait in line for a car. The simple idea of driving vehicles to their customers quickly spread across the country and became the Enterprise difference. It is one reason why Enterprise is consistently ranked one of the 50 best companies in the country to launch your career, ranked number one in customer service in its industry and has continued to grow in a very competitive arena. A seemingly small idea by one employee a long way from corporate headquarters launched relatively unknown Enterprise Rent-A-Car into a leader in their industry.

Assuming you have answered the first four questions for your team – they know what is REALLY important, they clearly understand how they are doing both individually and as a team, and they are confident that you care – your Butterfly Effect can come from answering the fifth question, "What difference do we make?"

Without any other leadership activity, your team will perform at a standard, baseline level. But when each person understands how their contributions make a positive difference to something greater than just their team, the game changes. Your team's results will be magnified because their mission is now far greater than themselves.

Achieving a larger, greater goal has a positive multiplier effect throughout the organization. People become energized, and customers become energized when they deal with energized people. Your results will reflect that energy. Once your Butterfly Effect gets started, you may well see results that you could never have forecasted.

Q: How do we affect other teams, and what is our impact on customers?

A: For the next several weeks, create an "awareness" exchange. Bring in people from other teams or departments and have them explain to your team what they do and how your team affects their team. In exchange, send one of your team members to that department to do the same.

If your team knows little about other departments in the organization (internal customers), they probably don't know much about their external customers, either. Help them understand by asking, "How does our team affect our customers' success?" Then, invite a customer to one of your team meetings and ask them to answer the same question. They will be glad to share how your team makes a difference to their business.

Answer the Fifth Question:
What difference do we make?

○ Your team wants to know what difference they make… what impact they have on the organization.

○ It doesn't matter what you say as an organization; what matters is what you do.

○ The more knowledge you share with your team, the more that knowledge can be multiplied throughout the organization. Don't let the 95/5 Rule "rule" your organization.

○ Everyone should be able to answer the questions: "What is our business?" and "How is business?"

○ The more informed your team is about the big picture, the better their decisions will be for the organization.

○ Pay attention to every idea…your Butterfly Effect could come from the most unexpected source.

> *When you answer the question,*
> *"What difference do we make?,"*
> *your people will become passionate promoters*
> *of your organization.*

Are you worth following?

"A leader is one who knows the way,
goes the way and shows the way."
– JOHN MAXWELL

Every leader dreams of answering The Magic Question, "How can I help?" But there is no magic wand you can wave to get your team to ask it. In fact, the question will likely never be asked unless you are the role model whom you want others to follow. People follow people. Your team follows you, and you must be worthy of being followed. If you are not willing to lead the pack, you need to move out of the way.

While your team may never directly ask you the question, "Are you worth following?," you can be sure that they are assessing you every day. Are you worthy of their loyalty, their trust and their discretionary effort?

Leadership is demanding. You are responsible for leading yourself as well as the team. If you want your team to consistently ask you The Magic Question, you have to be the very best.

The good news is that the rewards for being the best leader as opposed to an average leader are heavily skewed. People want to work for the best, buy from the best and deal with the best in almost every situation in our society. The best-selling books sell millions more copies than average books. The best movies generate millions more dollars than 50 average movies. Likewise, the rewards for being the best organization within your industry are enormous. Customers flock to winners. When you create an atmosphere where your team's needs are being met, they will choose to go above and beyond to make your organization the best.

I have discovered that there are five habits that separate the best leaders from average leaders:

1. The habit of communicating effectively

2. The habit of increasing knowledge

3. The habit of earning trust

4. The habit of being a little uncomfortable

5. The habit of giving back

These are personal habits that are required for your long-term success. If you adopt these five habits, you will become the kind of leader your team will be privileged to follow.

THE HABIT OF COMMUNICATING EFFECTIVELY

Connecting with your team and answering their questions is what this book is all about. My final point about communication is this: Good communication is a two-way street. You need to listen to your team just as much as you talk to them…if not more. You've probably heard the saying, "God gave you two ears and one mouth for a reason – so you can listen twice as much as you talk." Bottom line, the best leaders are the best listeners.

But there will be nothing for you to hear if your team isn't talking to you. And if they're not talking, there is a reason. Do your team members feel comfortable telling you the truth? Or do they think they have to tell you what you want to hear?

One of my favorite stories is the classic fable *The Emperor's New Clothes* by Hans Christian Andersen. As with all parables, the story about the vain and powerful Emperor has important lessons for us. You're probably familiar with Andersen's tale, but just in case you're not, the gist is that the Emperor goes naked in a parade because everyone is afraid to tell him the truth about his "new suit." It takes a small child to point out the obvious, but by then it's much too late to fix the embarrassing situation.

The moral of the story for leaders is that you shouldn't get so caught up in your own leadership position that you're afraid or unwilling to ask for or receive feedback. If your team is intimidated by the power of your position or feels pressure to conform to the majority, sooner or later you could end up like the Emperor and get caught in an embarrassing position. It is up to you to create an atmosphere in which your team knows without a doubt that honest feedback and suggestions are welcomed, without recourse.

THE HABIT OF INCREASING KNOWLEDGE

No matter what you want to accomplish, you will need more knowledge than you have right now. I'm not sure when or where I first heard, "The more you learn, the more you earn," but it was early in my business career. I probably discounted it as someone's attempt to be clever. But over the years, I've found that was some of the best advice I've ever received.

A great source of knowledge is learning from other people's experiences. No issue that you are facing is unique to you – others have already worked their way through the same problem. Learn from them. Find a mentor to guide you or look for a book on the subject. As the famous saying goes, "Only a fool learns from his own mistakes. The wise man learns from the mistakes of others."

Without question, the best way to learn more is to read more. A lot of people say they don't have time to read. That is simply not true. It's not a matter of time; it's a matter of priority. So the question is, should reading be one of your top priorities?

Let me ask you this: How many books do you think you need to read to be in the top 5 percent of all non-fiction readers in the world? Only one book per month! Reading one book per month means reading about half a chapter a day – maybe 10 or 15 minutes. Top 5 percent for a 10-minute-a-day investment? What a deal! If you can't find 10 minutes, start with a book on time management…you will find 10 minutes.

During the course of my career I've also discovered that the more knowledge you share, the more knowledge you gain. The best way to learn is to teach someone else. If you and your team together studied one book each month for one year, you would read, discuss and analyze 12 books. In five years, 60 books! You and your team would be more knowledgeable than any competitor.

Learning is contagious and energizing. Knowledge creates energy because you and everyone on your team will develop a thirst for learning even more. Knowledge shared is knowledge multiplied.

When you make learning a top priority, your team will become more confident and make better decisions for your organization.

You may be thinking, "I don't have the budget to provide books for everyone on my team." No problem. The beauty of knowledge is that it is readily available. You can purchase gently used books very inexpensively on the Internet, or you could borrow books for free from the library. Knowledge is everywhere, but it won't come looking for you...you have to search for it.

Q: How can we multiply our knowledge?

A: Take your team on a learning journey:

1. Provide each team member with a book (the same book) that is interesting and relevant to their success. The book should be brief and impactful.

2. During the week, every person should read the chapter that will be discussed the following week.

3. Dedicate 20 minutes every Monday (or the day most convenient for your team) to discuss the concepts from the applicable chapter.

4. Make a commitment to do something different based on the concepts presented in that chapter.

THE HABIT OF EARNING TRUST

The greatest single impact on effective leadership is trust. Trust is even more important than communication. People will go out of their way to avoid communicating with those they do not trust. If your team doesn't trust you, you are wasting each other's time.

Brian Tracy says, "Trust is the glue that holds all relationships together." So how can you make a habit of earning trust? It begins with your integrity. Trust, integrity and honesty are inextricably linked. To earn trust, you must be trustworthy. Are you open and honest? Do you do what you say you will do? When you commit to something, can your team "consider it done"?

If people perceive you to be a person of integrity, you will earn their trust over time. Someone once said, "People of integrity expect to be believed, and when they're not, they let time prove them right."

On the other hand, if you sacrifice your integrity, nothing else really matters. After all, does it matter what you say to people if they don't trust you? Does it matter how committed, optimistic, skilled at resolving conflicts or courageous you are if people do not trust you? None of these traits matter if you lose your team's trust. It simply makes no difference how great your intentions are. If there is little or no trust, there is little or no foundation for a successful relationship.

A key ingredient to establishing and maintaining your integrity is to discover and then face the real truth – not what you hope or want to be the truth, but the absolute reality of your situation. Ronald Reagan once said, "Don't be afraid to see what you see." Our nature is to be selective with the truth and to cling to beliefs that are pleasant to us. Seeking the real truth is an unnatural act, but one that is well worth doing.

What are the characteristics of people with integrity?

○ **They establish integrity as a top priority in their life.** They understand that their personal integrity is non-negotiable, and they make it the cornerstone of their actions and decisions.

○ **They have the courage to stand up for what they believe.** They have clear, uncompromised values and communicate them without hesitation.

○ **They do what is right regardless of the circumstances –** no hidden agendas, no games and no regrets. Martin Luther King, Jr. once said: "The ultimate measure of a man is not where he stands in moments of comfort and convenience, but where he stands in times of challenge and controversy."

○ **They never compromise their integrity by** rationalizing a situation as "an isolated incident." There are no "isolated incidents." They know where their integrity boundaries exist and stay within them.

○ **They never allow achieving results to become more important than the means to achieving them.** How they win is just as important as winning.

○ **They do what they say they will do.** They know their integrity is in question every time they say they are going to do something, regardless of how insignificant the commitment might be. They don't over-commit themselves or commit to something beyond their control. When they say they will do something, you can consider it done.

○ **They have a love of truth.** They choose to search for the truth and have the courage to confront reality. Jack Welch, former CEO of General Electric, calls the love of truth "the candor effect." He says that absolute candor "unclutters" conversations because everyone speaks the authentic truth rather than the political rhetoric that is so often heard in meeting rooms and boardrooms.

The people in your organization judge your integrity every day, not by what they hear you say, but by what they see you do. When you criticize one of your team members in public, you lose integrity. When you encourage your sales team to stretch the truth, your integrity comes into question. When you show favoritism, choose not to return phone calls, say you're out of the office when you're not, or say that you didn't receive a message when you did – you lose your team's trust. Of course, you probably wouldn't intentionally do most of these things, but our intentions really don't matter. What matters is what we do.

People judge your integrity on what they see...and they either see it or they don't. There are no varying degrees of integrity. You either have it or you don't. There is no such a thing as a minor lapse of integrity. The day-in-day-out, seemingly insignificant things that you do represent the greatest opportunity for integrity erosions. People don't forget integrity mistakes. They will forgive and forget most any judgment error, but integrity mistakes are forever.

Is there ever a time when a small, white lie is small enough that it doesn't really matter? Is there a point at which small lies are okay but big ones aren't? If so, where is that point...and how does your team know when they cross the line? The answer is that no lie is so small that it doesn't matter. As minor as a small lie may seem at the time, it has a lasting effect. You cannot pick and choose when you will be a person of integrity. You can't justify a white lie by thinking, "No one was hurt, so it's okay." Once you start making excuses, they will come a little easier each time, and soon you will find yourself on a slippery slope that can lead to an integrity meltdown.

If you want to be a leader who is worth following, you must be a leader of integrity. Then and only then will people follow you.

Ask *Yourself...*

Are you a leader with unquestionable integrity?

Your integrity is tested and revealed by the choices you make in the most challenging times. When those times arrive, give yourself the Personal Integrity Check by asking yourself these four questions:

1. Are my actions in sync with our organizational values?

2. How would I feel if this decision was shared in the news?

3. Would it be perfectly okay if someone made the same decision that affected me?

4. Is it the right thing to do?

THE HABIT OF BEING A LITTLE UNCOMFORTABLE

Success naturally makes you comfortable. You might not notice this in yourself, but it's easy to see in others, especially in sports. How many times have you watched teams take a lead, lose their momentum and then lose the game because instead of playing to win, they began playing not to lose? They pull back and start playing cautiously, losing the intensity that earned them the lead. Before long, their lead evaporates.

Being comfortable for too long can work against you. It's safe in the comfort zone – you know the boundaries, the landscape and the other comfortable players. There is little or no risk; a misstep here or there is not very costly. But nothing big is won in the comfort zone. Because the risk is small, so is the reward.

The comfort zone of success can also lead to complacency, and complacency is the root of mediocrity. When you become complacent with success, it won't be long before mediocrity takes over. You can't remain at the top without making a conscious effort to keep improving.

Early in my career, while working for Xerox, one of my yearly goals was to win the annual President's Club award. Each year, the top corporate performers were recognized with a great trip. After enjoying a couple of these President's Club trips, I observed that 80 percent (my estimate) of the winners were the same people every year.

Were all those repeat winners just the lucky salespeople with the best territories? Of course not. Many changed territories multiple times but still earned the President's Club award. Their "luck" was in making the choice to keep getting better, even though they were already at the top. In the years since that observation, I have confirmed that the winners who keep winning – in any organization – do so because they keep doing what is necessary to win. They keep learning and growing and forcing themselves out of their comfort zone.

Learning and growth occur when you are uncomfortable. Think of the defining moments of learning and growth in your life. Were you hanging out in your comfort zone? Probably not. I bet you were hanging over the edge.

If you feel yourself settling into a comfortable routine, ask yourself, "Am I getting complacent? Am I too comfortable?" Here is the acid test: If you can achieve your goals doing business as usual, your goals are not high enough. To raise your performance to the next level, set goals that make you worry and sweat – in other words, goals that make you a little uncomfortable.

You have to let go to grow. You have to be willing to purposely seek discomfort in a learning opportunity at the edge of your comfort zone. For most people, it's not natural to choose to be uncomfortable, but the best leaders do it anyway. Here are three questions to help you explore the edge of your comfort zone:

1. **Who else has done it?** You may think you are in uncharted territory, but it's unlikely that you are trying something no one has ever done. Whether your comfort zone ends at learning a new skill, speaking in public, coaching a tumbleweed employee or quitting a bad habit, find someone who has explored the same edge. That person can mentor you, support you and encourage you.

2. **What is the worst-case scenario?** Oftentimes our discomfort comes from fear about the unknown that lies beyond our comfort zone. Identify the worst possible outcome if you step out of your comfort zone. If you can live with that outcome, go for it.

3. **How great could it be?** Your dreams are usually bigger than your comfort zone. Focus on your dreams and let that passion magnetically draw you to the edge.

Ask Yourself...

Am I worth following?

Are you setting the right example? Is your attitude worth catching? Are you living up to your commitments? What do you stand for personally – what are your core beliefs? Has your integrity been tested and proven?

THE HABIT OF GIVING BACK

Leadership is about giving…of your time, your energy and your attention. All of your efforts are directed toward helping others grow. But that growth doesn't happen overnight. In fact, in some cases, you may never know how much you impacted the success of others.

Your team's growth may be similar to that of the exotic Chinese bamboo seed. When this particular seed is planted and nurtured, it can take up to two years for a sprout to break through the earth. It requires the right watering, sunlight, care and feeding to build a strong root structure and foundation for growth. However, once it breaks ground, the bamboo can grow over 100 feet in two weeks! The benefits of patience are abundant with this seed…just as they are with leadership patience.

Not too long ago while touring Boston, I passed a cemetery where Ephraim Wales Bull was buried. I had never heard of Ephraim Wales Bull, but the tour guide said he was the person who created Concord grapes. However, he never profited from the grapes because he died before they were marketed in jellies and jams.

The reason I share the story of Ephraim Wales Bull is because the epitaph on his gravestone reads, "He Sowed, Others Reaped." I think that should be our mission as leaders – to keep sowing and allow others to reap. That is what leadership is all about.

ANSWER THE SIXTH QUESTION:
ARE YOU WORTH FOLLOWING?

○ Your team is watching you every day to see if you are worthy of their loyalty, trust and discretionary effort.

○ The very best leaders develop five key personal habits:

1. The habit of communicating effectively – your team must know without a doubt that honest feedback and suggestions are genuinely welcomed.

2. The habit of increasing knowledge – the best way to learn more is to read more; knowledge shared with your team is knowledge multiplied.

3. The habit of earning trust – it doesn't matter what you say; it matters what you do.

4. The habit of being a little uncomfortable – seek discomfort in a learning opportunity at the edge of your comfort zone.

5. The habit of giving back – success as a leader is about growing other people.

When you answer the question, "Are you worth following?,"
your team will invest their time,
energy and efforts to follow you.

THE MAGIC QUESTION

"How can I help?"

*"Make people who work for you feel important.
If you honor and serve them, they'll honor and serve you."*
– MARY KAY ASH

Engaged, committed team members who willingly give discretionary effort…

Isn't that what we hope for as leaders? Isn't that everything we want, in a nutshell?

The good news is that you can have it! When you answer the six questions your team is asking, you will hear The Magic Question: "How can I help?"

Building a winning team begins with you, the leader, answering the questions we've talked about in this book. Sometimes you may wonder if it really matters if you answer all of the questions…

it does. If you try to skip any of the questions, it's like rolling a wheel with a section missing – you may arrive at your destination, but it will take a lot longer to get there and it won't be a smooth trip. On the other hand, when all of your team's needs are being met, you will reach your goals faster and easier and achieve better results.

Let the magic begin!

Four ways to bring
The Magic Question
into your organization

1. *The Magic Question* PowerPoint™ Presentation

Introduce and reinforce *The Magic Question* to your organization with this cost-effective, downloadable PowerPoint™ presentation. Includes facilitator guide and notes.

Contact www.CornerStoneLeadership.com $99.95

2. Keynote Presentation

Invite author David Cottrell to inspire your team and help create greater success for your organization. Each presentation is designed to set a solid foundation for both organizational and personal success.

Contact Michele@CornerStoneLeadership.com.

3. *The Magic Question* Workshop

Facilitated by David Cottrell or a certified CornerStone Leadership instructor, this three- or six-hour workshop will reinforce the principles of *The Magic Question*. Each participant will develop a personal action plan that can make a profound difference in their life and career.

Contact Michele@CornerStoneLeadership.com.

4. CornerStone's dynamic new **manager training program**. An in-depth six month development process including assessments, coaching, and all the resources needed to equip new managers for success. Contact www.services.CornerStoneLeadership.com.

The Magic Question Package $99⁹⁵

(A Savings of 36%)

$14.95 $16.95 $15.95 $14.95 $14.95

$9.95 $9.95 $15.95 $10.95 $12.95

Other books by David Cottrell

☑ YES! Please send me extra copies of *The Magic Question*!

1-30 copies $14.95   31-100 copies $13.95   100+ copies $12.95

| *The Magic Question* | _____ copies X _____ | = $ _____ |

| *The Magic Question* PowerPoint™ (downloadable product) | _____ copies X $99.95 | = $ _____ |

Additional Leadership Development Resources

| *The Magic Question* Package (As shown on page 94.) | _____ pack(s) X $99.95 | = $ _____ |

Other Books

_____	_____ copies X _____	= $ _____
_____	_____ copies X _____	= $ _____
_____	_____ copies X _____	= $ _____
_____	_____ copies X _____	= $ _____

	Shipping & Handling	$ _____
	Subtotal	$ _____
	Sales Tax (8.25%-TX Only)	$ _____
	Total (U.S. Dollars Only)	**$ _____**

Shipping and Handling Charges

Total $ Amount	Up to $49	$50-$99	$100-$249	$250-$1199	$1200-$2999	$3000+
Charge	$7	$9	$16	$30	$80	$125

Name _____ Job Title _____

Organization _____ Phone _____

Shipping Address _____ Fax _____

Billing Address_____ Email _____
(Required for downloadable products)

City_____ State _____ ZIP _____

❑ Please invoice (Orders over $200) Purchase Order Number (if applicable) _____

Charge Your Order: ❑ MasterCard   ❑ Visa   ❑ American Express

Credit Card Number _____ Exp. Date _____

Signature _____

❑ Check Enclosed (Payable to: CornerStone Leadership)

Thank you for reading *The Magic Question!*

We hope it has assisted you in your quest for personal and professional growth. CornerStone Leadership is committed to providing new and enlightening products to organizations worldwide.

Our mission is to fuel knowledge with practical resources that will accelerate your team's productivity, success and job satisfaction!

Best wishes for your continued success.

CornerStone
Leadership Institute

www.CornerStoneLeadership.com

Start a crusade in your organization –
have the courage to learn, the vision to lead,
and the passion to share.